A Leader Without Followers? The United States in World Politics after Bush

Barry Buzan

July 2009

About the Author

Barry Buzan is Montague Burton Professor of International Relations at the London School of Economics and Political Science, Honorary Professor at the Universities of Copenhagen and Jilin, and a Fellow of the British Academy. Among his recent books are *The United States and the Great Powers: World Politics in the Twenty-First Century* (Polity, 2004), and, with Lene Hansen, *The Evolution of International Security Studies* (Cambridge University Press, 2009).

‘We seek your leadership. But if for some reason you are not willing to lead, leave it to the rest of us. Please get out of the way.’

Kevin Conrad
representing Papua New Guinea
Bali Conference, December 2007[1]

A Leader Without Followers? The United States in World Politics after Bush

Introduction

During the second half of the 20th century, the United States (US) was without question an outstandingly successful leading power. It took over leadership of the West during the Second World War, and used that victory to bring Western Europe and Japan into the democratic sphere, in the process solving the German problem. It made the democracies more numerous, secure and powerful than ever before.[2] It then led the West in the long and eventually successful struggle against the Soviet Union over whether industrial society would be organised on the principles of capitalist liberal democracy or centrally-planned totalitarianism. During the Cold War, the United States was instrumental in transforming some of the key practices of international relations, mainly within the Western camp, but increasingly beyond it. In particular, the US promoted a twin revolution by spreading the market as the organising principle for the world economy, and multilateralism as the expected way of conducting the business of the society of states. Crucial to this liberal revolution was a vast increase in the number and functions of both intergovernmental organisations (IGOs) and international non-governmental organisation (INGOs) as the forums in which the global economy was managed and the practice of multilateral diplomacy pursued. Within the overarching framework of the Cold War, with its bipolar balance of power and omnipresent threat of nuclear incineration, the market and multilateralism steadily transformed the international relations of the world outside the communist bloc. By creating global trade and financial regimes, the US pushed the threat of great power wars and balance of power behaviour among the Western states and their allies to the margins. Nowhere was this transformation more obvious than in Western Europe, where the US mainly promoted the rise of what has now become the European Union (EU), so creating an expanding sphere of post-Westphalian international politics in what had once been the cockpit of world wars. From the late 1970s, well before the end of the Cold War, China embarked on a sustained process of 'reform and opening up' linking its internal development to participation in the US-led global market economy. After 1990 the Soviet Union gave up the struggle to construct an alternative to capitalism, and the transformation that had been underway for several decades became effectively global with only a few minor holdouts such as Iran and North Korea. The US was an effective leader not only because it promoted liberal economic and political values that were attractive to many others, but also because it was prepared to bind its own power in multilateral rules and institutions sufficiently that its followers could contain their fear of its overwhelming power.[3]

While all true, these accomplishments should not give the impression that this was some sort of friction-free golden age for US leadership. There were intra-allied disputes aplenty within NATO, and all of the US's other alliances, and trade and financial negotiations were often fractious and protracted. There were big, but not fatal disasters, most obviously the Vietnam War, and glaring hypocrisies in the contrast between the US's rhetoric about human rights and democracy, and its practical support for repressive dictatorial regimes in Latin America, Africa and Asia. Where there was tension between liberal values and anti-communism, US governments generally favoured supporting the latter. Given the ideological nature of the Cold War, the US was widely despised on the political left not just for its particular behaviours (Vietnam, the nuclear arms race, antagonism to Cuba, Chile, support for anti-leftist military actions in many places) but also because of what it was: the principal backer and beneficiary of a globalising capitalism. Although it enjoyed widespread respect and admiration for its politics, economy, technology and culture, the US was far from universally loved even by many of those outside the left. Despite these negatives, the US did win the Cold War, did succeed in spreading liberal economic values widely (much less so with respect to liberal social and political values), and did strengthen the society of states by equipping it with an unprecedented array of multilateral and transnational institutions. It remained in principle (though not always in practice) committed to multilateralism, and because of that commitment was able to create a zone of peace in the capitalist core that defied the predictions of both Realists and Marxists.

Since the late 1990s, however, and very sharply since 2003, the US has in many ways become the enemy of its own 20th century project. It has explicitly downgraded, or sometimes rejected altogether, its commitment to multilateralism, and turned against many of the intergovernmental organisations that it was instrumental in creating.[4] In the absence of any great power challenger it has pursued an increasingly imperial and militarised foreign policy[5], continued to engage in 'unnecessary wars',[6] and maintained an unprecedented relative level of military expenditure exceeding that of the next dozen military powers combined. Even before the economic crunch of 2008 it had retreated from leadership on trade, lost ground as the undisputed financial leader, and become an obstacle to most attempts to tackle global warming. By its use of torture, and even more so the public advocacy of such interrogation techniques by senior administration figures, and by its rejection of the Geneva Conventions on prisoners of war, it exposed itself to ridicule and contempt as an advocate for human rights. It has instead, during much of the Bush administration, projected a rhetoric and practice of sovereigntism and unilateralism, and celebrated its own power, particularly military power. The effect of all this has been increasingly to unravel the self-binding of earlier decades and to undermine the loyalty of the US's followers, particularly, but not only, in Western Europe.[7] During these years the US came frequently to be seen more as part of the problem than as part of the solution.

Because the Bush administration was so widely reviled outside (and in its final years also, at last, within) the US, there is room for the thought that the Bush administration was some kind of ghastly aberration, and that the election of Barack Obama represents a return to normal. While I certainly do not wish to deny that the Obama administration represents a very major shift of style, and up to a point substance, from the Bush one, I nevertheless think that there is also room for the argument that shifts are underway that are much bigger than those represented by particular administrations. Some of these are internal to the US[8] and some reflect structural and political changes in the world as a whole. One has to consider the change represented by the Obama administration against this background of larger movements that provide the environment in which the US under any leadership now has to operate. This is not just about the poisoned chalice left by the Bush administration for its successor (though that too), but also about the broader shape of world politics.

From this perspective, there are three vital questions about the future of US leadership:

- Will the US want to continue to play the role of world leader in the coming decades?

- If it does, will it be able to continue its past success in attracting and holding followers?

- Will the issues likely to dominate international politics in the coming decades tend to strengthen or weaken the attractiveness and legitimacy of US leadership?

The next section answers 'probably yes' to the first question and 'probably no' to the second. The section following reviews six issues likely to be prominent on the agenda of world politics and argues that most, if not all, of these will probably work against the maintenance of US leadership in anything like the form it had during the last half of the 20th century. The conclusions look at the structural causes eroding US and Western hegemony, and at the consequences of this for the management of international society.

The US as a World Leader

Will the US continue to want to be world leader, and if it does, will it be able to sustain its Cold War success in attracting and holding followers? There are few reasons to doubt that the US has the military capacity to lead, and that even if this is likely to be eroded by rising powers, will retain that capacity for some decades. On this I agree with Robert Singh.[9] There is, however, a major question mark over how relevant this key area of US strength will be in the coming decades. In the absence of great power wars, having a military advantage may count for less than it once did in the stakes of global leadership. It may, indeed, raise again the spectre of 'over-stretch' that Paul Kennedy made fashionable two decades ago, where great powers dissipate their strength by diverting too many resources to the military.[10] As the US itself has demonstrated clearly over the past half century, it is economic and ideological power that count more towards leadership quality and legitimacy. And in the wake of the US having led itself and the rest of the world into what looks like the deepest economic crisis since the 1930s, there have now to be more questions about the economic foundations of US leadership. Not only is the US now hugely burdened with debt and a dysfunctional economic system, but one of the central planks of its ideological legitimacy, the Washington consensus, has imploded almost as dramatically as the Soviet Union and its bureaucratic, totalitarian, modernist alternative to liberal capitalism, and may well be damaged beyond repair. Despite this development, and as is obvious from the behaviour and rhetoric of the new Obama administration, there are good reasons to agree with Singh[11] that the US will want to continue in its global leader role. One indicator of this is its ongoing willingness to sustain a military budget more or less equal to that of the rest of the world combined despite the fact that it no longer has a serious military rival. Such expenditure underpins the US's claim to be the sole superpower, and thus the only member of an exclusive club of one entitled to claim special rights in relation to the management of international society. Sole superpower status also creates a certain demand pull for leadership. Americans are by no means alone in thinking of themselves, as President Bill Clinton put it, as the 'indispensable nation' when it comes to questions of world order and global management.[12] Although, as witness the International Criminal Court and the Kyoto Environmental agreements, the US does not have a veto, US leadership or opposition can make or break the kinds of collective action that are possible for international society. Responding collectively to crises is more difficult without US leadership and resources. Underpinning this demand pull from outside is a habit of leadership now engrained into US institutions and self-image for more than 60 years. That habit is internally supported by those strong elements of American exceptionalism fired by the idea that the US forms of polity (democracy), economy (capitalism) and society (individualism) represents the right and inevitable future for all of humankind. As Simon Bromley puts it: 'nearly all strands of American nationalism share the view that the United States is a unique power whose national interest is more or less synonymous with the global interest.'[13] This self-perception was greatly reinforced by victory in the Cold War and the subsequent emergence of the US as the sole superpower. It should not be forgotten that the ending of the Cold War represented not just the defeat of the Soviet challenge, but the final ideological victory of liberal capitalism over its fascist and communist rivals as flag-bearer for modernity. One should also not forget that the US is still a revolutionary state, and that the messianic elements of US foreign policy reflect not just the strong religiosity of its society, but also its very much alive revolutionary tradition. More instrumentally, there is a longstanding awareness amongst US elites that their own and the country's prosperity and stability depend on the international trade and finance arrangements that absorb its surplus production,[14] and more recently that fund its deficits and keep its consumer prices low.

Yet although the probability is that the US will continue to want to be world leader, one needs to keep in mind two possible counter-arguments. The first is that a really costly failure, most obviously the disaster in Iraq, could fuel a desire to retreat from the burdens and pains of leadership. The second is the possibility of return to the long tradition of political isolationism that dominated US foreign policy before the Second World War.[15] These two elements could easily reinforce each other. American exceptionalism can cut both ways. The revolutionary tradition can support messianic, proselytising, engagement with the world of the kind pushed by neocons, but it is also open to the attractions of the more utopian line of revolutionary thinking that wishes to preserve the purity of the revolution by isolation, and which limits the obligation of the revolution to teaching by force of example rather than by interventionist attempts at conversion. A resounding defeat for engagement could make isolationism, probably in the form of 'offshore balancing' a more saleable option in US electoral politics.[16] So too could the effects of the current economic crisis, particularly if they strengthen those who call for protectionism to keep jobs and investments in the US. As the example of the 1930s illustrates, despite its disposition towards outward looking economic engagement, the US is not beyond turning to protectionism in a crisis. It is noteworthy how many commentators make the point that the US is more likely to be driven out of its superpower status by the unwillingness of its citizens to support the role than by any failure on the material front.[17] If there is also failure on the material front, which would put domestic interests more into zero-sum rivalry with overseas engagements, the incentives for such sentiments will increase. This logic is visible in the nationalist reactions to the current economic crisis, and how to keep recovery benefits with the US.

If the US remains willing to lead, will anyone follow? I will examine this question more closely in the next section, but the general point is the extent to which shared values and visions between the US and its followers have already declined, particularly across a widening Atlantic. Partly this was to do with the turn to unilateralism and the conspicuous abandonment of commitments to multilateralism and self-binding under the Bush administration noted above. A good symbol of this was the replacement of talk about 'friends and allies' or 'the free world' with a much harsher and more instrumental line about 'coalitions of the willing'. This rhetorical shift seemed to abandon any US interest or belief in long-term friendships and alliances, and replace it with a purely calculated logic of immediate and specific shared interest. Although key institutions of the West, such as the North Atlantic Treaty Organisation (NATO), still exist, they have been largely pushed to the margins of where the action is in global high politics. Anti-Americanism, though obviously not new,[18] became exceptionally strong under Bush. Cold War anti-Americanism was based mainly on ideological grounds and as such provided the foundations for friends, allies and followers of the US as well as for its enemies, supporting the creation and maintenance of shared identities on both sides. The anti-Americanism of the early 21st century is more culturally based, and more corrosive of shared identities. It questions whether an unsustainable 'American way of life' is an appropriate model for the rest of the world, and whether the US economic model is either sustainable or desirable. It looks at health (obesity) and welfare (tens of millions without medical insurance) issues; at a seeming US inclination to use force as the first choice policy instrument; at the influence of religion and special interest lobbies in US domestic politics; at a US government which under Bush was openly comfortable with the use of torture and was re-elected; and at a federal environmental policy until recently in denial about global warming; and asks not just whether the US is a questionable model, but whether it has become a serious part of the problem. While some of this was specific to the Bush administration, and is being turned around by Obama, some of the deeper issues are more structural. The US is much more culturally conservative, religious, individualistic, and anti-state than most other parts of the West. Its religion and cultural conservatism and anti-statism set it apart from most of Europe, while its individualism and anti-statism set it apart from Asia.

This kind of anti-Americanism is based on very real differences, and corrodes the very foundations of what 'the West' used to mean. Indeed, it raises the possibility that the idea of 'the West' was just a passing epiphenomenon of the Cold War.[19]

Although one should never underestimate the capacity of the US for renewal, innovation and re-invention, there is no doubt that the two terms of the Bush administration have asset-stripped half-a-century of respect for, goodwill towards and trust in US leadership. And it is far from clear that all this can just be blamed on the Bush administration, and hope therefore vested in a 'return to normal' now that it has exited from office. The Bush administration certainly had its unique idiosyncracies, but it also reflected, and helped to consolidate, a shift in the centre of gravity of US politics.[20] There are certainly welcome changes of style and rhetoric in the Obama administration, but it is much less clear that there will be changes of substance big enough and wide-ranging enough to restore the legitimacy of US leadership. Certainly Obama is uniquely favoured with the personal and rhetorical skills to undo some of the damage done by the Bush administration. But there are limits to what any American President can do both at home and abroad, and the economic implosion has sharply reduced the resources available to the new administration for world leadership, both materially and in terms of the ideological legitimacy of the Washington consensus. The Obama administration cannot just go back to the late 1990s and pick up from where Clinton left off. It faces a transformed world that needs to invent new rules of the game.

How will all this carry forward into the issues that are likely to dominate world politics in the coming decades?

Six Challenges for US Leadership

I have already ventured far into the hazardous (but fun, and intellectually stimulating) realms of futurology, and am about to go further in, so now is the time to register the usual caveats about the perils of prediction in world politics. Michael Cox rightly likes to quote Harold Macmillan's line about 'events, dear boy, events' as a good antidote to the pretensions of International Relations scholars who think they can tell what the future will look like. Events – think of the breakup of the Soviet Union, 9/11, or the collapse of the banking system – have a way of derailing such prognostications. So what follows is on 'other things being equal' terms, even though they may turn out not to be. I pick six areas which on the bases of past momentum and present dynamics will probably be central to the question of US leadership, and ask whether others are likely to follow where the US is likely to go.

The Global War on Terrorism (GWoT)

I have argued at length elsewhere[21] that the GWoT is unlikely to provide an issue anything like comparable to the Cold War in sustaining and legitimising US leadership, and I will not repeat all of that here. The gist of it is that 'terrorism' offers no political alternative to the West comparable to that generated by the Soviet Union; that the costs of the GWoT include serious threats to the values it is supposed to be defending, and that counter-terrorism may be effective enough to keep the threat to acceptable levels. In addition, the securitisation of terrorism, while having had some success, is vulnerable to competing securitisations such as the rise of China. The main caveat to that argument is if terrorists raise their game very considerably from the levels we have seen to date, either by mounting more spectacular attacks (using Weapons of Mass Destruction (WMD) for example) or by increasing the number and frequency of attacks. If that happens, then the GWoT could become a durable macrosecuritisation[22] like the Cold War, and the US might well be able to use it to sustain leadership over a broad group of followers. But if things go on as they have done since 9/11, then terrorism will probably not be seen as a sufficiently large threat to sustain the costly and controversial apparatus of the GWoT. This is one key point on which I disagree with Singh.[23]

To be clear, I am *not* arguing that the threat from terrorism is inconsequential or temporary. In my view, the threat from terrorism is, and will remain for the long term, a significant problem for the type of society in which we now live. One part of this problem, and not the biggest, is the hugely counterproductive effect of US policies in the Middle East, which appear to have served as an effective recruiting sergeant for the likes of Al Qaeda.[24] This means that the West will have to face threats from Islamic extremists for at least a generation or two, possibly longer. The bigger part of the problem is that pointed to by Martin Rees,[25] which is that in this phase of human development, large powers of destruction are becoming ever more easily and widely available to ever smaller groups of people. Partly this is to do with evolving technologies for causing damage, and partly to do with the structural vulnerabilities of ever larger, more densely packed and more interdependent human populations. It used to take great power-sized human collectivities to construct major means of destruction such as large armies, fleets of bombers, or nuclear weapons. Now quite small groups, or in the case of toxins, and viruses (whether biological or digital) even individuals, can create and use instruments of great destructive power. Even primitive nuclear capabilities might be constructed by fairly small groups. How societies are to preserve and manage liberal values when disaffected minorities can access such threats is a massive political question that takes one well beyond the immediate concerns of the GWoT. Current concerns about terrorism are merely a harbinger of this growing problem about the relationship between political order and the means of violence.

If threats of this sort are to be responded to with endless 'long wars', then, as we have already seen with the effect of the GWoT on the domestic politics of the US, liberal values will be corroded by the very measures taken to defend them. If the response to terrorism is constructed in terms of criminality rather than war, then open civil societies will have to adjust to terrorism by accepting a certain level of disruption and casualties as the price of openness, freedom and civil liberties. This would take considerably more political maturity than is normally found in Western democracies, but the fact that Europeans and Americans find it acceptable that 50,000 of their fellow citizens should die on the roads each year suggests that such tolerance for threats of structural violence is not unrealistic. If this is the way to go, then on performance to date, European societies, which have displayed a much calmer and more measured response to terrorism, are much more likely to provide the model for how to deal with this threat than is the US. But the key point here is that terrorism is unlikely to remain the dominant issue for international leadership. Concerns with terrorism will remain, but the GWoT will probably not become the new Cold War in the sense of providing a durable macrosecuritisation that structures world politics, and legitimises US leadership over a period of several decades.

The Rise of China

For the US, an increasing securitisation of China as a threat to the US position as sole superpower is perhaps the development most likely to erode US commitment to the GWoT. It is not possible to have two dominant securitisations, so the more the US focuses on China, the less priority the GWoT will get, perhaps sliding down to niche securitisation status alongside the 'war on drugs'.

The main argument here is that it seems almost certain that the steady drumbeat of concern in Washington about rising China as a peer competitor will get louder as China does indeed grow in power. This drumbeat is longstanding and deeply rooted.[26] To the extent that Realist thinking, with its emphasis on material factors, dominates in Washington, and the US retains its existing commitment to being the sole-superpower and not allowing any challengers, then a rising China *must* appear threatening to the US. Since it is the mere fact of China's rising power that drives this concern, it will make little difference in Washington whether China rises 'peacefully' or not. But this question of the nature of the China that rises will be crucial to whether others share US perceptions of China as a threat.

If a rising China becomes ultra-nationalist, aggressive and militarist, then it could well be that others would share US perceptions and so provide followers for US leadership. But the Chinese leadership is well aware of this danger, and determined to avoid the mistakes made by Germany, Japan and Soviet Union in their rising period.[27] If they can carry off their design for a 'peaceful rise' then it becomes entirely possible that US perceptions of China as threatening will not be shared widely if at all. Those many voices currently in opposition to US hegemony, and speaking of the need for a more multipolar world order, might well welcome China's rise. If China is relatively benign in the sense of not using violence against its neighbours, and staying broadly within the rules of the global economic order, Europe will not care much about its rise, and will not feel threatened by it. Russia is a more complicated case, because it is one of China's neighbours, and has worries about Chinese designs on the sparsely populated territories of the Russian far east. Yet the two countries have developed a quite stable strategic partnership,[28] have many useful economic complementarities, share an interest in non-intervention and regime security, and may well want to continue to bandwagon with China against the US. India is also a complicated case, having to balance a growing economic relationship with China against some lingering territorial disputes and a desire not to be overshadowed in status terms by China. Unless China turns nasty and threatening, India will probably try to continue to play the US and China against each other as it does now, leaving the main economic and political costs of balancing China to the US.[29]

The big question mark is Japan, which since the end of the Cold War has not only maintained, but somewhat strengthened its alliance with the US, and whose relationship with China remains deeply clouded by unsettled legacies from Japan's invasion of China during the 1930s and 1940s. A considerable weight of expert opinion thinks that Sino-Japanese relations are underneath their formal political correctness, bad, and on the level of society and pubic opinion getting worse, with both governments in different ways to blame.[30] If China's rise is benign, but the US securitises it anyway, Japan will face very difficult choices. If it stays with the US, it would find itself in the uncomfortable position of being the front line in a new Cold War between Washington and Beijing. That might not look attractive compared with the options of either resolving the history problems and bandwagoning with China or following India into a more independent, middle-ground position between Washington and Beijing. Japan is the toughest problem facing China's 'peaceful rise' strategy.

Whatever the room for debate about timing, there is a high probability that China will rise significantly in the coming decades. There is also a high probability that the

US will remain keen to maintain its number one status and so will find this threatening. But if China conducts its rise peacefully, this US concern will be a parochial one, shared by few, possibly none, of the other great powers. In this case the US will be a leader with few, or possibly no, followers. And since China is, for its own reasons, broadly on board with the GWoT, there is no scope for the US to try to link 'the China threat' to the terrorist one. China's rise is likely to overshadow the GWoT, and if China plays its hand cleverly, it could put the US more on its own than it has been since before the First World War.

The Middle East

Disagreements over policy in the Middle East already rank as one of the conspicuous areas of disaffection between the US and Europe, and this seems likely to continue.[31] There is no doubt that the Middle East is a profound mess and likely to remain so. This mess is deep-rooted and has many causes, both internal and external, that I do not have the space to go into here. The main point for the question of future US leadership is that many of the US interventions into the Middle East, both those of the Bush administration and those more longstanding, are widely perceived to have been counterproductive, not only feeding the terrorist problem but also deepening the many tragedies in the region. The occupation of Iraq in 2003 looks set to generate far more, and bigger, problems than it has solved. More or less unconditional US support for Israel is a perennial Washington idiosyncrasy. It has strong support from the Israel lobby and the US religious right, but inspires little enthusiasm elsewhere, and has so far hamstrung the US from pushing decisively towards a two-state solution to the Israel-Palestine problem. The Obama administration's more robust line on the necessity of a two-state solution is welcome, but faces such daunting obstacles (a divided and fractious Palestinian leadership, an Israeli leadership with deep ties to the settlers, and an aggressive and mischief-making leadership in Iran) that its chances of making much headway do not look promising. This festering sore has grown steadily worse, with Israel creating ever more difficult facts on the ground, and assisting in the self-destruction of a coherent Palestinian negotiating partner. US support for the Saudi regime helps keep in power a government whose domestic deals with Wahabi Islamists recycles large sums of oil money into the support of Islamic fundamentalism, though here it has to be said that Europeans are just as culpable. Perhaps only on the question of preventing the proliferation of WMD, on which more below, does US policy in the Middle East enjoy much support, but even that is undermined by the hypocrisy of the US turning a blind eye to Israel's construction of a substantial nuclear arsenal while seeking to forbid Arab states and Iran from acquiring their own deterrents.

The basic point here is that except on the WMD issue, US policy in the Middle East is unlikely to attract followers. After the Iraq fiasco, even ever-faithful Britain would have trouble joining in. Russia, China and increasingly India have their own interests in the region that are often competitive with those of the US. Like China, Japan is interested mainly in the supply of oil, and cares little about Middle East politics because it assumes, probably rightly, that almost any owner of the oil would want and need to sell it. From this point of view, the only worry is that some one power might obtain a monopoly on Middle Eastern oil and thus be able to control the price. Given both the deep divisions and antagonisms in the Middle East, and its effective fragmentation by the West,[32] the possibility of such a monopoly looks remote. The US tie to Israel looks unlikely to change and will continue to poison Washington's position in the region. Bad US policies and competing interests in the region from other powers provide no foundations for US leadership. Again, the Obama administration inherits such a poor situation from its predecessor, which was pretty much content to give Israel a free hand, that it is far from clear that there is much scope for attempting to resolve the situation. Neither Israel not the Palestinians seem prepared to negotiate, with extremists ascendant on both sides.

Liberal Values

One of the foundations of US legitimacy as world leader in the six decades since the end of the Second World War has been its support for liberal values. To simplify a very complicated topic, the US has championed political liberal values in the form of democracy and human rights, and economic liberal values in the form of free(r) trade, and financial liberalisation. There has always been a very substantial element of hypocrisy in this which should not be ignored. During the Cold War the US often favoured anti-communists over democrats, and treated democratic India more as an enemy than as a friend (while arming its military-ruled rival Pakistan). More was done in relation to human rights, but not where these got in the way of the market or anti-communism. Much was done for opening up trade and finance, but the US protected good parts of its own economy (most notoriously agriculture, although again the Europeans and Japanese are no better), and exploited the advantages that holding the global reserve currency gave it in relation to trade deficits and inflation. Yet even so, much was done. Democracy was supported in some places, barriers to global trade and finance were stripped away to a very significant degree, and human rights were established as an issue on the international agenda.

At this point, however, there is little scope left for US leadership on liberal issues, either social or economic. On the social side, the GWoT means that Washington is still under pressure to prefer anti-terrorist governments to democratic ones. US abuses of human rights in Iraq (Abu Ghraib) and the GWoT (Guantanamo Bay, its policy of 'extraordinary renditions', and a seeming US government acceptance of torture), and its fierce resistance to the International Criminal Court, have gutted Washington's credibility to say much about human rights. The Obama administration will no doubt take a much more politically liberal line than its predecessor, but it has a huge amount of damage to repair before it can even attempt to reassert US leadership in this area. And on this issue at least the EU does not need US leadership and is happy to take its own lead as a 'civilian power'.

In terms of economic liberalism the Obama inheritance is even worse. Under Clinton and Bush, the financial world took on a globalised life of its own, seemingly needing less of US leadership. Even before the current economic crisis, competitors to the dollar as reserve currency were on the rise, and US indebtedness was weakening its ability to lead. On trade, the US had largely ceased to lead anyway, its weakening economic position making it more protectionist. Obama's options are hugely constrained by the magnitude of the economic crisis. It is not clear that he is an economic liberal, and even if he is, many of his Party in Congress look likely to be even less enthusiastic about further trade liberalisation (except in bilateral arrangements favourable to the US) than the Bush Republicans were. World trade is imploding, and although international cooperation to deal with the economic crisis is in some ways impressive, this situation does not provide much opportunity for US leadership. The US led the world into this recession, and what is obvious even at this early stage is that the US, badly damaged itself, cannot lead the world out of it. It has neither the economic resources, nor, with the collapse of the Washington consensus, the ideological authority to do so. What is already becoming clear is that if the world economy can be managed globally at all, it will have to be done collectively (for example via the G20 and other similar groups of leading powers), giving bigger voices to other players. With the Washington consensus discredited, other ideas about how to run the global political economy are in play, both European social markets, and the Beijing consensus.[33] The truth of Bromley's observation made before the 2008 collapse has been amplified by recent events: 'US economic leadership power exists but it is a wasting asset.... governance of the world economy is something that would have to be accomplished collectively if it is to be accomplished at all.'[34] If attempts to get the global economy going again fail, or are too protracted and costly, then the emergence of a more regionalised world political economy becomes more likely, again a scenario that narrows the scope for US leadership (as will be elaborated below).

The Environment

Environmental issues are the wild card of international relations. They could generate crises in many different forms (climate change; sea level change; the rapid spread of fatal or disabling diseases; the poisoning effects of the man-made chemical bath in which we now all live; the rising price of food; rocks from space crashing into the planet; and so on). These crises might arrive tomorrow, or ten or a hundred years from now, or (less likely) they might never arrive, so it is hard to tell when they will make their impact. It is also difficult to predict the effects of some of these. There may be technical fixes for some of them, such as vaccines and space missions to change the course of incoming asteroids or comets. Even global warming and sea level rise might be subject to technical fixes, though this is a much more daunting challenge, and quite probably one loaded with its own dangerous side-effects. Environmental issues represent the 'events' problem for prediction in spades. When (or if) they do arise, they could easily dominate the international agenda, radically changing political priorities and quickly pushing more traditional problems into the background. On some of these issues, the US would, because of its strong technological position, be an obvious leader. That seems likely to be true if the news was that a large asteroid or comet was going to collide with Earth in a few decades time, and perhaps also if disease control was the issue. On global warming, however, the commitment of Americans to a high consumption lifestyle, and the federal government's longstanding resistance to serious pollution controls, has, in the eyes of many, already defined the US more as part of the problem than as the solution. The Obama administration has certainly changed the rhetoric on this, but how much policy change it can manage remains to be seen.

The impact of the environmental wild card on the question of US leadership is thus extremely difficult to predict. Certain kinds of developments could rescue US leadership and put it back into the driving seat. Here the Obama administration might make a difference. Under the Bush administration, with its commitment to the oil industry, and its consequent denial that global warming was a problem, pollution and global warming added to the general disaffection with the US that eroded its leadership standing. Obama's enthusiasm for green energy as a fix for both the environment and the economy might well restore US credibility in this area. It is less clear that there is any fix for the problem of the unsustainable American lifestyle, and the loss of respect for the US as a model for the rest of the world. Yet even here one should not underestimate the capacity of the US for reinventing itself. Odd combinations of religious takeup of environmental stewardship, corporate interests in eco-profits, technological innovation, and local and national politics generating new approaches to environmental management could yet put Washington back on top in relation to climate change.

Weapons of Mass Destruction

Preventing the proliferation of WMD, particularly nuclear weapons, may be one other issue on which the US still has some leadership potential. Even here, however, things are in pretty ragged shape. The non-proliferation regime has always been dogged by its core hypocrisy that a few countries are allowed to have nuclear weapons and the rest forbidden.[35] Of late there has been a shift from a mainly consensual approach aiming for universal support to a more elitist one in which the US and its followers actively try to prevent new entrants to the nuclear club while hanging on to their own nuclear privileges. This approach amplifies the hypocrisy, and necessarily attracts narrower support. Its attractiveness is also undermined by the inconsistency of US policy: small sticks and big carrots to North Korea; a blind eye to Israel; big sticks and small carrots to Iraq and Iran; offers of collusion to India once proliferation has occurred; and, after a policy of mainly sticks, a seemingly confused acceptance of Pakistan. US ability to lead on this issue is seriously and negatively entangled with its mainly unpopular position in the Middle East. The Proliferation Security Initiative has nevertheless been a success, and this issue looks to be one in which the US will continue to find some followers in relation to specific cases (most obviously North Korea and Iran).[36] Given the confusion and inconsistency in US policy, its leadership cannot be more than local and tactical.

Conclusions

On most of the six big issues just surveyed, the argument suggests that it is unlikely that the US will be able to recover the sort of global strategic leadership status it enjoyed between 1945 and 2003. The main caveats to this conclusion are that a major escalation of terrorist activity, or certain kinds of environmental crisis might revive US leadership, but neither can be counted on, and it would not be difficult for either to exacerbate the already compromised US position on these issues.

If the era of US leadership is winding down, what will replace it? As I have argued at length elsewhere,[37] no immediate replacement is available as far out as the next couple of decades, and so I agree with Robert Singh[38] that an alternative global leader is not on the cards. Only China and the EU are likely to have the material capability, but China is unlikely to have the legitimacy and the EU is unlikely to have either the political and military capacity or the will. The US will almost certainly retain sufficient military capability to play the leadership role, and as argued will probably, but not certainly, retain the will. The problem is that its economic position is weakened, and the legitimacy of US leadership is now severely corroded, which is what creates the possibility of a leader without followers. If this loss of legitimacy had simple causes one might hope to fix it, but unfortunately it does not. This is the key weakness of Singh's argument, which discounts the social side of the US position, and puts too much emphasis on the material factors. The legitimacy of US leadership was certainly degraded by the policies and style of the Bush administration, and there could be few people better qualified than Obama to begin repairing this damage, perhaps to a significant extent. But in addition to the constraints posed by the economic crisis, there are three additional barriers in the way of any project to revive the legitimacy of US leadership post-Bush.

First, and simplest, is the growing range of policy disagreements on specific issues between the US and others. As surveyed in this paper, there is some hope that under Obama this will improve in specific areas, though many areas of disagreement are likely to remain, some deep.

Second, and related, is the growing disjuncture between how the US perceives itself and how the rest of the world sees it. Partly this is about the decay of the US as a model for others. Partly it is about the chronic inability of the US to see itself as others see it. The long and deeply-established tendency of the US to see itself as an intrinsic force for good because it stands for a right set of universal values, makes it unable easily, or possibly at all, to address the disjuncture between its self-perception and how others see it.[39] As both Ian Clark and Andrew Hurrell argue, self-righteous unilateralism, does not acquire legitimacy abroad. To the extent that celebrations of US power as a good in itself (because the US is good) dominate American domestic politics, this does not inspire the US to seek grounds for legitimating its position abroad.[40] A contributing factor here is the US tendency to demand absolute security for itself.[41] The problem for the US of transcending its own self-image is hardly new, but it has become both more difficult and more important in managing its position in a more complex world in which the US is no longer neither so clearly on the right side of a great struggle, nor so dominant in material terms. Although the liberal democratic world surely has much to be grateful for to the US during the 20th century, memories are short, and the US lacks grand crusades like the contests against fascism and communism to underpin its leadership and mask the excesses of American exceptionalism. Despite the hopes of some for a 'long war' against terrorism, the GWoT is unlikely to become the new Cold War. As the sole superpower, a hegemonic US thus needs to work harder to find legitimacy. Yet it remains in thrall to its own power and a perception, now less widely shared abroad than for a long time, of its own virtue. It is unclear at this point whether Obama will be able to transcend this aspect of American politics, though what is clear is that the nature of American politics makes it difficult for any president to do so.

The third aspect of the legitimacy deficit is the most difficult to fix. It stems not from any particular characteristic of the US, but from the material and social aspects of sole-superpower hegemony: from the very fact of unipolarity itself. As both AdamWatson and Clark argue, since decolonisation global international society has developed a growing disjuncture between a defining principle of legitimacy based on sovereign equality, and a practice that is substantially rooted in the hegemony of great powers.[42] The problem is the absence of 'a satisfactory principle of hegemony – rooted in a plausibly wide consensus'[43] with which international society might bridge this gap between its principles and its practices. Because the US is the sole superpower, this problem has come into particularly sharp focus. A concentration of power in one actor, as Clark observes, disrupts the ideas of balance and equilibrium that are the traditional sources and conditions for legitimacy in international society.[44] This problem would arise for any unipolar power, but it connects back to the second, US-specific, aspect of the legitimacy deficit in two linked ways. Under the Bush administration, the US lost sight of what Watson calls *raison de système* ('the belief that it pays to make the system work'), and this exacerbated what is anyway the illegitimacy of hegemony in itself.[45] David Calleo argues that, Obama notwithstanding, for the US 'hegemony is likely to remain the recurring obsession of its official imagination, the idée fixe of its foreign policy', and as Stefano Guzzini notes, 'US primacy that is not embedded in a legitimate world order undermines US security'.[46] Thus a circle closes in which US obsessiveness about its own national security, and aspiration to make it absolute, helps to undermine the international legitimacy of its position, which is part of what makes it insecure.

All of this points not to an alternative leader taking the place of the US in some kind of hegemonic transition, but to a world with either no superpowers,[47] or no global leader. Such a world would still have several great powers influential within and beyond their regions: the EU, Russia, China, Japan, the US, possibly India. It would also have many substantial regional powers such as Brazil, South Africa, Turkey and Iran. Singh casts this as 'apolarity' and dismisses it as unworkable and undesirable.[48] But there is more room for argument about that than he allows. Whether one sees a move towards a more polycentric, pluralist, and probably regionalised, world political order as desirable or worrying is a matter of choice. For those who focus on the improvement and extension of global governance, the weakening of US leadership and the de-centring of international society would appear to be a serious backward step. But for those who think that the tensions among a rampant global economy, a weak interstate society and a humankind still deeply divided by identities laid down centuries or millennia ago, are becoming too great to handle, some retreat from the ambitions of globalisation might be welcome.[49] Perhaps global governance has been too ambitious an aim at this stage of human history, with the attempt creating more management problems than current human social and political capacities are able to solve. A less ambitious world order, with regions looking after themselves more might well remain peaceful and involve fewer frictions and failures.

Whatever its merits, a more regionalised world order would, however, mark a retreat from universalist liberal agendas of both a political and an economic sort. Smaller states and peoples within regions that looked more after themselves would be at risk of becoming the vassals of their local suzerain power(s), having little or no recourse to outside help or support. The global market would weaken, local great powers would have more say in their regions, and promoters of cultural and political diversity would be freer to go their own way, and define their own meanings for human rights, sovereignty, non-intervention and democracy. This might all be quite manageable at the global level given that ideological differences would be far less than during the 20th century. Given the restraining effects of both nuclear weapons, and the great increase in the ability of peoples to resist foreign occupation, regions and their associated great powers might be happy to cultivate their own affairs rather than seeking global dominance. Such an arrangement might also be a reasonable way of finding a transition from the unsustainable high tide of Western global domination that peaked in the 20th century, and began to ebb after the Second World War. One downside is that it would probably leave zones of chaos and/or conflict in parts of Africa and the Middle East where no local powers are strong enough to provide regional order, disputes are many, and local groups often armed and ready to fight. Another would be the while some kinds of global management problems could be reduced by moving towards a more decentred world order, the big question mark would be over whether and how a diffuse, pluralist international society could handle planetary problems such as those likely to come from the environment.

Given the steady diffusion of power into Asia, in part stimulated by Western policy, the emerging multicultural world order cannot easily meet Watson's and Hurrell's desire for the acceptable principle of hegemony that would legitimise either US or Western leadership. In such a world, hegemony by *any* one power or culture will be unacceptable. Hegemony may well work regionally as a way of dealing with the equally unsustainable extreme of sovereign equality, itself already slipping into question as the numbers of failed states and *de facto* protectorates and mandates rises. But it cannot work globally, or at least not beyond the capacity and willingness of all of the major powers to undertake collective global management responsibilities on specific issues. In this perspective the whole question of the sustainability or not of US leadership begins to look less relevant. The US may hasten or delay its own exit from leadership. But the waning of the Western tide, and the re-emergence of a more multi-centred (in terms of power and wealth) and more multicultural (albeit with substantial elements of Westernisation) world, mean that hegemonic global leadership whether by a single power or the West collectively is no longer going to be acceptable. The question is whether the new world order will express itself mainly in regional hegemonies, or whether it can find the foundations for a much more pluralist kind of collective great power hegemony than anything seen so far in world history.[50]

Notes

1 http://news.wired.com/dynamic/stories/B/BALI_CLIMATE_CONFERENCE?SITE=WIRE&SECTION=HOME&TEMPLATE=DEFAULT – accessed 24 Dec. 2007.

2 Duedney, Daniel H. (2007) *Bounding Power*, Princeton, Princeton University Press, 183-5.

3 Ikenberry, G. John (2001) *After Victory: Institutions, Strategic Restraint and the Rebuilding of Order After Major Wars*, Princeton, Princeton University Press; Ikenberry, John G. (2002) 'Multilateralism and U.S. Grand Strategy', in Stewart Patrick and Shepard Forman (eds) *Multilateralism in U.S. Foreign Policy*, Boulder CO., Lynne Rienner, 121-40.

4 Crossette, Barbara (2002) '"Killing One's Progeny": America and the United Nations', *World Policy Journal* 19(3): 5-9.

5 Bacevich, Andrew J. (2002) *American Empire: the Realities and Consequences of U.S. Diplomacy*, Cambridge MA., Harvard

University Press; Guzzini, Stefano (2002) 'Foreign Policy Without Diplomacy: The Bush Administration at a Crossroads', *International Relations* 16(2): 291–7.

6 Harper, John L. (2005) 'Anatomy of a Habit: America's Unnecessary Wars', *Survival*, 47(2): 57-86.

7 Chace, James (2003) 'Present at the Destruction: The Death of American Internationalism', *World Policy Journal*, 20(1): 1-5; Daalder, Ivo H. and James M. Lindsay (2003) *America Unbound: The Bush Revolution in Foreign Policy*, Washington DC, Brookings Institution Press; Buzan, Barry (2004) *The United States and the Great Powers: World Politics in the Twenty-First Century*, Oxford, Polity, 2004, 151-95; Prestowitz, Clyde P. (2003) *Rogue Nation: American Unilateralism and the Failure of Good Intentions*, New York, Basic Books; Layne, Christopher (2006) 'The Unipolar Illusion Revisited: The Coming End of the United States' Unipolar Moment', *International Security*, 31(2): 7-41.

8 Kupchan, Charles and Peter Trubowitz (2007) 'Dead Center: The Demise of Liberal Internationalism in the United States', *Interntional Security*, 32(2): 7-44.

9 Singh, Robert (2008) 'The Exceptional Empire: Why the United States Will Not Decline - Again', *International Politics*, 45(5): 571-93. For a more sceptical view see Kupchan, Charles A. (2002) *The End of the American Era: US Foreign Policy and the Geopolitics of the Twenty-first Century*, New York, Alfred Knopf.

10 Kennedy, Paul (1989) *The Rise and Fall of the Great Powers: Economic Change and Military Conflict from 1500 to 2000*, London, Fontana.

11 Singh, 'The Exceptional Empire'.

12 Clinton, William J. (1997) 'Inaugural Address', http://www.presidency.ucsb.edu/ws/print.php?pid=54183 (accessed 2 Dec. 2007).

13 Bromley, Simon (2008) *American Power and the Prospects for*

International Order, Cambridge, Polity, 46. See also: Fukuyama, Francis (1992) *The End of History and the Last Man*, London, Penguin.

14 Bender, Thomas (2006) *A Nation Among Nations: America's Place in World History*. New York, Hill and Wang, 183-245.

15 Though how this tradition plays into US politics is complicated. See Dunn, David Hastings (2005) 'Isolationsim revisited: seven persistent myths in the contemporary American foreign policy debate', *Review of International Studies* 31(2): 237-61.

16 Layne, Christopher (1997) 'From Preponderance to Offshore Balancing: America's Future Grand Strategy', *International Security* 22(1): 86-124; Layne, 'The Unipolar Illusion Revisited'.

17 Calleo, David (1999) 'The United States and the Great Powers', *World Policy Journal* 16(3): 11-19; Kapstein, Ethan B. (1999) 'Does Unipolarity Have a Future?', in Ethan B. Kapstein and Michael Mastanduno (eds) *Unipolar Politics: Realism and State Strategies After the Cold War*, New York, Columbia University Press, 468, 484; Lake, David A. (1999) 'Ulysses's Triumph: American Power and the New World Order', *Security Studies* 8(4): 78; Kapstein, Ethan B. and Michael Mastanduno (eds) (1999) *Unipolar Politics: Realism and State Strategies after the Cold War*, New York, Columbia University Press, 14-20; Haass, Richard N. (1999) 'What to Do With American Primacy', *Foreign Affairs*, Sept./Oct. (web offprint, 12 pp.); Spiro, Peter J. (2000) 'The New Sovereigntists: American Exceptionalism and Its False Prophets', *Foreign Affairs*, 79(6): 9-15.

18 Katzenstein, Peter J. and Keohane, Robert O. (eds) (2006) *Anti-Americanisms in World Politics*, Ithaca, Cornell University Press.

19 Calleo, David (2004) 'The Broken West', *Survival* 46(3): 29-38; Clark, J. C. D. (2004) 'Is There Still A West? The Trajectory of a Category', *Orbis* 48(4): 577-91; Kupchan, Charles A. (2006) 'The Fourth Age: The Next Era in Transatlantic Relations', *The National Interest* 85: 77-83.

20 Kupchan, 'The Fourth Age'.

21 Buzan, Barry (2006) 'Will the 'global war on terrorism' be the new Cold War?', *International Affairs* 82(6): 1101-18.

22 On the concept of macrosecuritisation, see: Buzan, Barry and Ole Wæver (2009) 'Macrosecuritization and Security Constellations: Reconsidering Scale in Securitization Theory', *Review of International Studies*, 35(2): 253-76.

23 Singh, 'The Exceptional Empire'.

24 Allin, Dana H. (2004) 'The Atlantic Crisis of Confidence', *International Affairs* 80(4): 649-63; Wilkinson, Paul (2005) 'International Terrorism: the Changing Threat and the EU's Response', *Chaillot Paper 84*, Institute for Security Studies, Paris.

25 Rees, Martin (2003) *Our Final Century*, London, William Heinemann.

26 Betts, Richard K. (1993-4) 'Wealth, Power and Instability: East Asia and the United States after the Cold War', *International Security* 18(3): 34-77; Christensen, Thomas J. (2001) 'Posing Problems without Catching up: China's Rise and Challenge for US Security Policy', *International Security* 25(4): 5-40; Ross, Robert S. (1999) 'The Geography of Peace: East Asia in the Twenty-first Century', *International Security* 23(4): 81-118; Roy, Denny (1994) 'Hegemon on the Horizon? China's Threat to East Asian Security', *International Security*, 19(1): 149-68; Shambaugh, David (1996) 'Containment or Engagment of China? Calculating Beijing's Responses', *International Security*, 21(2): 180-209; Ward, Adam (2003) 'China and America: Trouble Ahead?', *Survival*, 45(3): 35-56.

27 Buzan, Barry (2009) 'China in International Society: Is "Peaceful Rise" Possible?', unpublished paper, 13 March.

28 Ferdinand, Peter (2007) 'Sunset, Sunrise: China and Russia Construct a New Relationship', *International Affairs*, 83(5):

841-67; Wilkins, Thomas (2008) 'Russo-Chinese Strategic Partnership: A New Form of Security Cooperation?', *Contemporary Security Policy*, 29(2): 358.

29 Buzan, *The United States and the Great Powers*, 107-31; Bromley, *American Power*, 151.

30 Drifte, Reinhard (2000) 'US Impact on Japan-China Security Relations', *Security Dialogue*, 31(4): 449-62; Dreyer, June Teufel (2006) 'Sino-Japanese Rivalry and Its Implications for Developing Nations', *Asian Survey*, 46(4): 538-57; Foot, Rosemary (2006) 'Chinese Strategies in a US-hegemonic Global Order: Accommodating and Hedging', *International Affairs*, 82(1): 77-94; Gries, Peter Hays (2005) 'China's "New Thinking" on Japan', *China Quarterly*, 184, 831-50; Li, Rex (1999) 'Partners or Rivals? Chinese Perceptions of Japan's Security Strategy in the Asia-Pacific Region', *Journal of Strategic Studies*, 22(4): 1-25; Mochizuki, Mike M. (2007) ' Japan's Shifting Strategy toward the Rise of China', *Journal of Strategic Studies*, 30(3/4): 739-76; Reilly, James (2004) 'China's History Activists And The War Of Resistance Against Japan: History in the Making', *Asian Survey*, 44(2): 276-94; Roy, Denny (2005) 'The Sources and Limits of Sino-Japanese Tensions', *Survival*, 47(2): 191-214; Rozman, Gilbert (2002) 'China's Changing Images of Japan 1989-2001: the Struggle to Balance Partnership and Rivalry', *International Relations of the Asia Pacific*, 2(1): 95-129; Tamamoto, Masaru (2005) 'How Japan Imagines China and Sees Itself', *World Policy Journal*, 22(4): 55-62; Yahuda, Michael (2002) 'The Limits of Economic Interdependence: Sino-Japanese Relations', unpublished m/s.

31 Boukhars, Anouar and Steve A. Yetiv (2003) '9/11 and the Growing Euro-American Chasm over the Middle East', *European Security* 12(1): 64-81.

32 Lustick, Ian S. (1997) 'The Absence of Middle Eastern Great Powers: Political "Backwardness" in Historical Perspective', *International Organization* 51(4): 653-83; Buzan, Barry and Ana Gonzalez-Pelaez (eds) (2009) *International Society and the Middle East*, Basingstoke, Palgrave.

33 Ramo, Joshua Cooper (2004) *The Beijing Consensus*, London, Foreign Policy Centre.

34 Bromley, *American Power*, 82.

35 Walker, William (2000) 'Nuclear Order and Disorder', *International Affairs*, 76(4): 725-39.

36 Valencia, Mark J. (2005) *The Proliferation Security Initiative: Making Waves in Asia*, Adelphi Paper 376, London, International Institute for Strategic Studies.

37 Buzan, *The United States and the Great Powers*.

38 Singh, 'The Exceptional Empire'.

39 Daalder and Lindsay, *America Unbound*, 194; Bender, *A Nation Among Nations*; Prestowitz, *Rogue Nation*, 1-17; Layne, 'The Unipolar Illusion Revisited'; Bromley, *American Power*, 46.

40 Clark, Ian (2005) *Legitimacy in International Society*, Oxford, Oxford University Press, 227-43; Hurrell, Andrew (2002) '"There Are No Rules" (George W. Bush): International Order After September 11', *International Relations*, 16(2); Hurrell, Andrew (2007) *On Global Order*, Oxford, Oxford University Press, 227-43.

41 Hendrickson, David C. (2002) 'Towards Universal Empire: The Dangerous Quest for Absolute Security', *World Policy Journal* 19(3): 1-10; Prestowitz, *Rogue Nation*, 273-4.

42 Watson, Adam, (1992) *The Evolution of International Society*, London, Routledge, 319-25; Watson, Adam, (1997) *The Limits of Independence: Relations Between States in the Modern World*, London, Routledge; Clark, Ian (1989) *The Hierarchy of States:*

Reform and Resistance in the International Order, Cambridge, Cambridge University Press.

43 Clark, *Legitimacy in International Society*, 254.

44 Ibid., 227-43.

45 Daalder and Lindsay, *America Unbound*, 195; Watson, *The Evolution of International Society*, 14.

46 Calleo, David P. (2008) 'The Tyranny of False Vision: America's Unipolar Fantasy', Survival, 50(5): 61–78; Guzzini, 'Foreign Policy Without Diplomacy', 296.

47 Buzan, *The United States and the Great Powers*, 132-46.

48 Singh, 'The Exceptional Empire'.

49 Kupchan, Charles A. (1998) 'After Pax Americana: Benign Power, Regional Integration, and the Sources of Stable Multipolarity', *International Security* 23(2): 40-79.

50 A much earlier version of this paper was presented to a seminar of the Global Policy Institute of the London Metropolitan University on 8 November 2007 and the text may be found on the Institute's website. A much extended version was published under the same title in *International Politics*, 45:5 (2008): 554-70, in which it was paired with an article by Singh (cited in Note 9) that took a mainly opposite view. This version, completed in mid-June 2009, looks at the argument approaching one year on after the transition from Bush to Obama.

www.ingramcontent.com/pod-product-compliance
Lightning Source LLC
LaVergne TN
LVHW050947080826
845145LV00004B/1444

* 9 7 8 1 9 0 7 1 4 4 9 9 8 *